I0902013

NATURAL DISASTERS Where I Live

BLIZZARDS

Tracy Vonder Brink

A Stingray Book

SEAHORSE PUBLISHING

Teaching Tips for Caregivers and Teachers:

This Hi-Lo book features high-interest subject matter that will appeal to all readers in intermediate and middle school grades. It may be enjoyed by students reading at or above grade level as well as by those who are looking for age-appropriate themes matched with a less challenging reading level. Hi-Lo books are ideal for ELL readers, too.

Each book appeals to a striving reader's age and maturity level. Opportunities are provided for students to read words they already know while encountering a limited number of new, high-interest vocabulary words. With these supports in place, students will read more fluently while increasing reading comprehension. Use the following suggestions to help students grow as readers.

- Encourage the student to read independently at home.
- Encourage the student to practice reading aloud.
- Encourage activities that require reading.
- Establish a regular reading time.
- Have the student write questions about what they read.

Teaching Tips for Teachers:

Before Reading

- Ask, "What do I know about this topic?"
- Ask, "What do I want to learn about this topic?"

During Reading

- Ask, "What is the author trying to teach me?"
- Ask, "How is this like something I already know?"

After Reading

- Discuss how the text features (headings, index, etc.) help with understanding the topic.
- Ask, "What interesting or fun fact did you learn?"

TABLE OF CONTENTS

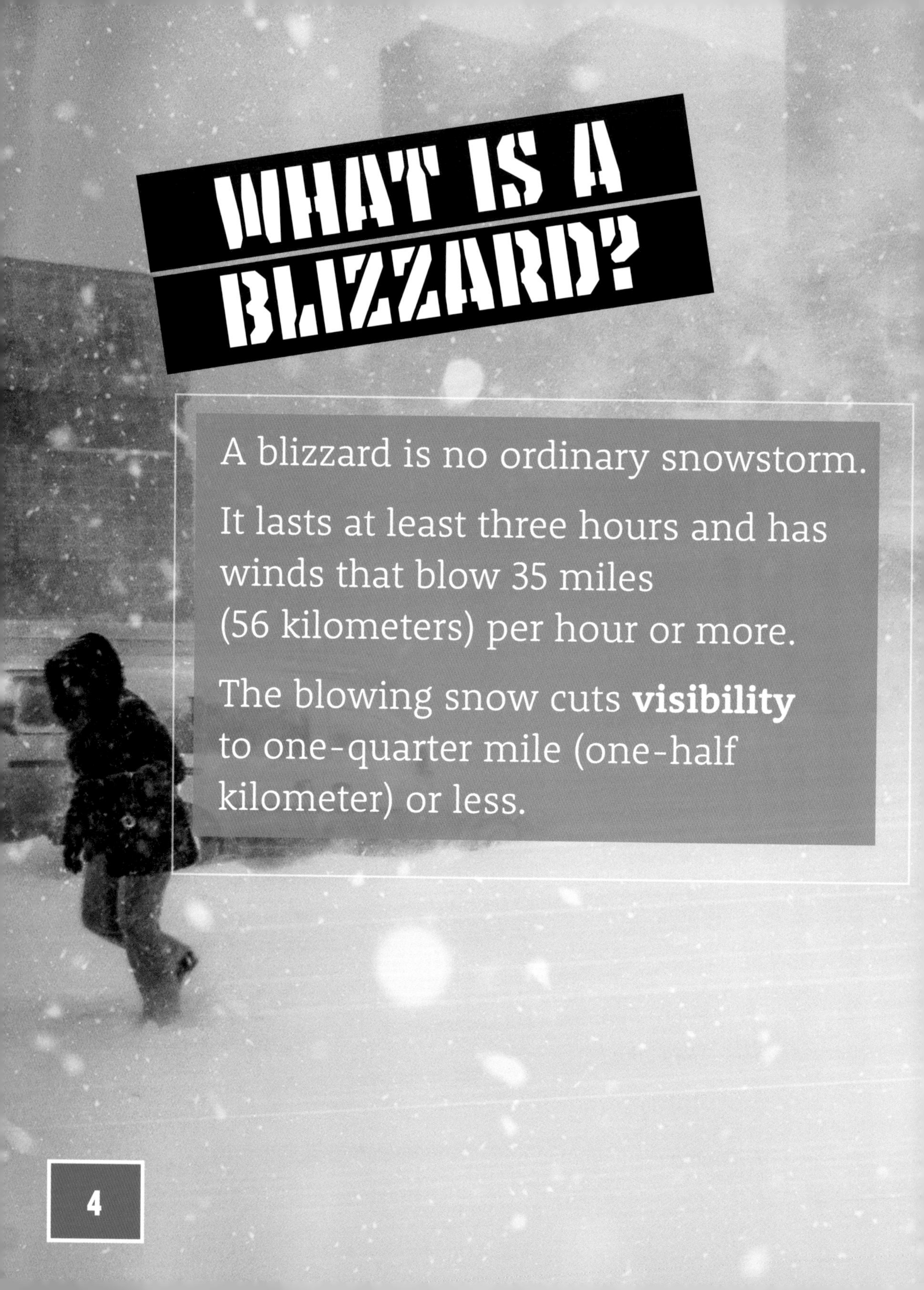

WHAT IS A BLIZZARD?

A blizzard is no ordinary snowstorm.

It lasts at least three hours and has winds that blow 35 miles (56 kilometers) per hour or more.

The blowing snow cuts **visibility** to one-quarter mile (one-half kilometer) or less.

FROZEN FACT

Low visibility makes it easy to get lost outside during a blizzard. People have died just a few yards away from the safety of their homes.

HOW DO SOME BLIZZARDS FORM?

Blizzards begin with storm clouds.

Warm and cold **air masses** meet to make these clouds.

The lighter warm air rises above the heavier cold air. Winds form.

Freezing temperatures in the air turn the cloud's **water vapor** to snow.

Wind and snow combine to form the blizzard.

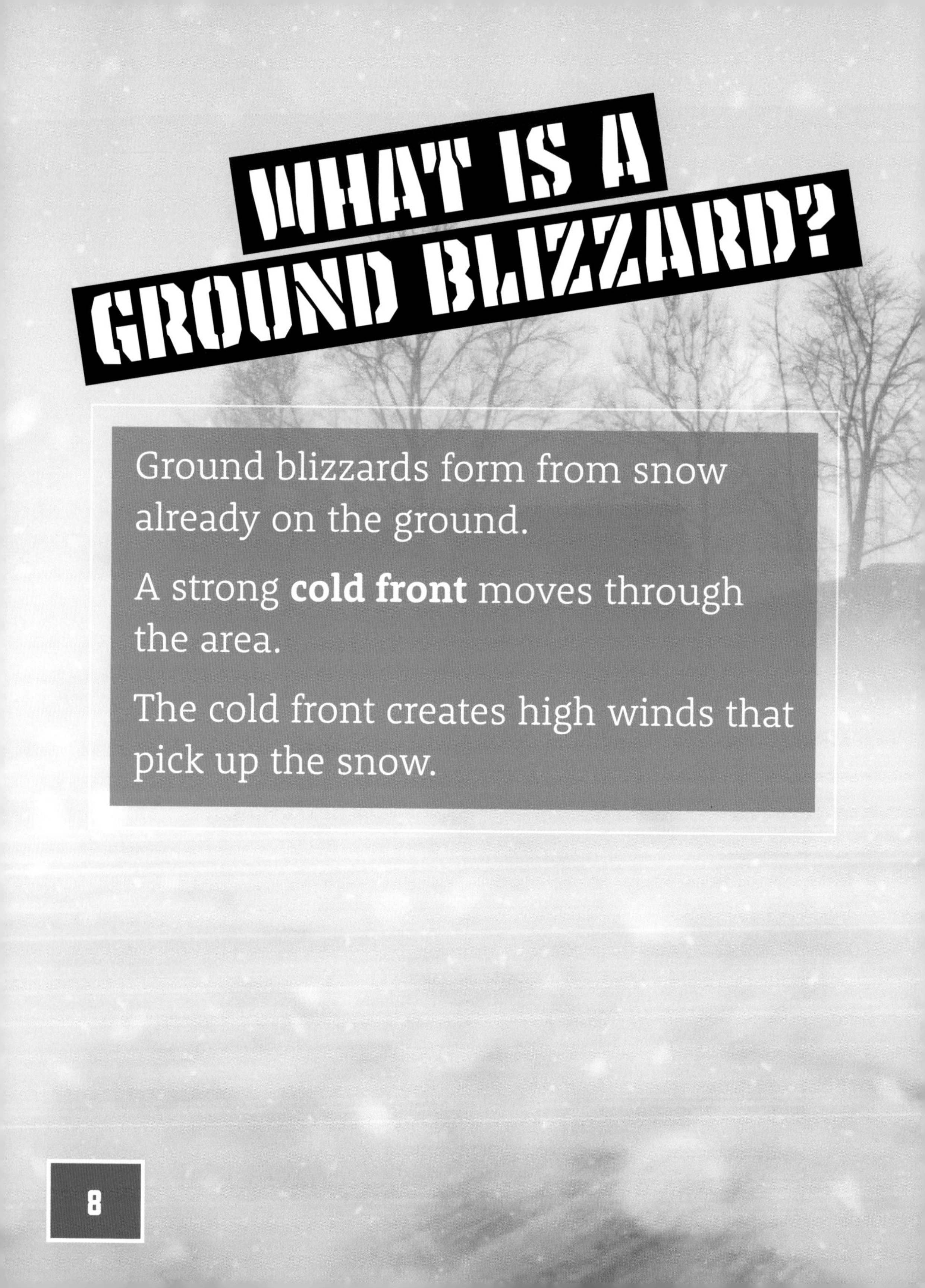

WHAT IS A GROUND BLIZZARD?

Ground blizzards form from snow already on the ground.

A strong **cold front** moves through the area.

The cold front creates high winds that pick up the snow.

In the nor'easter of March 2018, winds reached up to 93 miles (150 kilometers) per hour in Massachusetts.

FROZEN FACT

A nor'easter is a storm that begins along North America's eastern coast. Nor'easters are strongest from September to April and have caused some of the worst blizzards in the United States.

WHERE DO BLIZZARDS HAPPEN?

A blizzard can happen almost anywhere in the world.

Parts of Canada, Russia, and China often have blizzards. So do Japan, Iran, and the United Kingdom.

Blizzards happen everywhere in the United States except along the California and Gulf of Mexico coasts.

In 2008, winter storms in China killed at least 129 people.

FROZEN FACT

Parts of the Northern Plains have more blizzards than the rest of the United States. This area has so many blizzards that it has been nicknamed "Blizzard Alley."

WHY IS A BLIZZARD DANGEROUS?

Drifting snow blocks roads and causes car accidents.

Blowing snow can become a **whiteout** that makes it impossible to see. People caught outside lose their way.

The extreme cold causes **frostbite** and **hypothermia**.

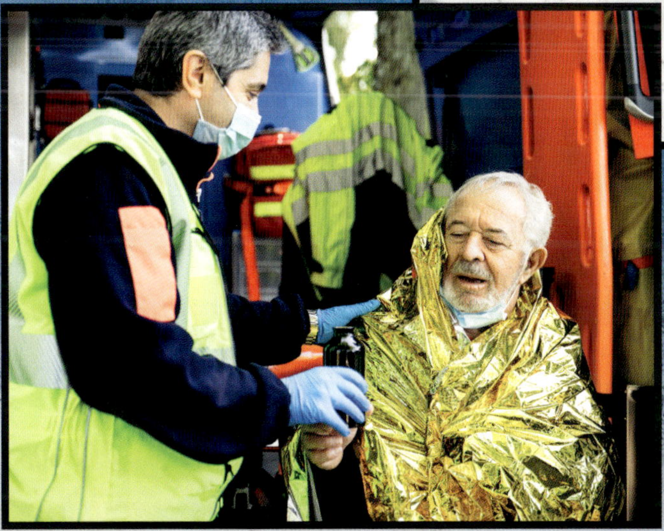

WHAT DAMAGE CAN A BLIZZARD DO?

A blizzard's high winds sometimes knock out power and heat.

Water pipes may freeze and burst in the cold.

Heavy snow may cause roofs to collapse.

FROZEN FACT

Blowing snow can create mounds called snow drifts. Some snow drifts have been measured at 50 feet (15.2 meters) tall.

THE WORLD'S DEADLIEST BLIZZARD

The Iran Blizzard of 1972 lasted a week.

It dumped as much as 26 feet (7.9 meters) of snow that buried entire villages in the country of Iran.

About 4,000 people died in the below-zero temperatures that came with the heavy snow.

1. Rescue party at Huron, bound together by ropes, searching for missing children. **2.** A schoolmistress compels a pupil to walk all night to prevent freezing. **3.** Another brave teacher shelters one of her pupils from the storm.

FROZEN FACT

The Children's Blizzard of 1888 was one of the deadliest blizzards in the U.S. It killed 235 people, including children on their way home from school.

PREDICTING A BLIZZARD

Weather satellites and **radar** track storm fronts.

Computers help analyze the information.

Forecasters look at all the data and decide if a blizzard is likely.

They send out a blizzard warning online, on TV, and on the radio when conditions are right.

The North American Blizzard of 1996 paralyzed the East Coast of the U.S. and cost three billion dollars in damages.

STAYING SAFE DURING A BLIZZARD

Gather emergency supplies such as food, water, blankets, and flashlights when a blizzard warning goes out.

Plan to stay indoors and do not try to travel.

If the power goes out, keep warm with layers of clothing and blankets and wear a hat and mittens indoors.

WINTER BLIZZARD
PREPARE FOR THE WORST & HOPE FOR THE BEST!
1. Shovel -Snowblower
2. Generator, Gasoline
3. Snow Tires
4. Protect water pipes
5. Flashlights
6. Batteries, Solar Charger
7. Salt or Sand
8. Boots, Gloves, Hat, Scarf
9. Ice Scraper
10. Fill Gas Tank
11. Stock up on non-perishables & water

GLOSSARY

air masses (air MA-suhz): large bodies of air

cold front (kohld fruhnt): the zone where a cold air mass is replacing a warm air mass

frostbite (FRAWST-bite): damage done to part of the body by freezing

hypothermia (hye-puh-THUR-mee-uh): a serious condition caused by dangerously low body temperature

radar (RAY-dahr): a way to find things by reflecting radio waves off them and receiving the reflected waves; *radar* is an abbreviation for radio detection and ranging

visibility (viz-uh-BIL-i-tee): the distance a person can see as a result of weather conditions

water vapor (WAW-tur VAY-pur): water in the form of a gas

whiteout (WITE-owt): a blizzard that reduces visibility to almost zero

INDEX

AFTER READING QUESTIONS

1. How long must a snowstorm last to be called a blizzard?
2. What is a ground blizzard?
3. What can happen to drivers during a blizzard?
4. How can blizzards damage buildings?
5. What tools help forecasters predict blizzards?

About the Author

Tracy Vonder Brink loves true stories and facts. She has written more than twenty books for kids and is a contributing editor for three children's science magazines. Tracy lives in Cincinnati, Ohio, with her husband, two daughters, and two rescue dogs.

Written by: Tracy Vonder Brink
Design by: Under the Oaks Media
Editor: Kim Thompson

Library of Congress PCN Data
Blizzards / Tracy Vonder Brink
Natural Disasters Where I Live
ISBN 978-1-63897-476-5(hard cover)
ISBN 978-1-63897-591-5(paperback)
ISBN 978-1-63897-706-3(EPUB)
ISBN 978-1-63897-821-3(eBook)
Library of Congress Control Number: 2021953379

Printed in the United States of America.

Photographs/Shutterstock: Alex Stemmer: cover(top); faboi: cover(bottom); Big Stories Production: p. 4-5; ffly: p. 6-7; RossEllet: p. 8-9; NOAA: 9(top); moderndest: p. 9(bottom); ZhangYueYang: p. 10-11; Lemanna: p. 12-13; Dmitry Kochergin: p. 13(top); Vadym Zaitser: p. 13(middle); loreanto: p. 13(bottom); JaCrispy: p. 14-15: SaPhoteg: p. 15; LOC:. 17; Salajean: p. 18-19; NOAA: p. 19; diy13: p. 20-21; snapphotos: p21

Seahorse Publishing Company
www.seahorsepub.com

Published in the United States
Seahorse Publishing
PO Box 771325
Coral Springs, FL 33077

SEAHORSE PUBLISHING